THE BIG BOOK OF MONACO FACTS

AN EDUCATIONAL COUNTRY TRAVEL PICTURE BOOK FOR KIDS ABOUT HISTORY, DESTINATION PLACES, ANIMALS AND MANY MORE

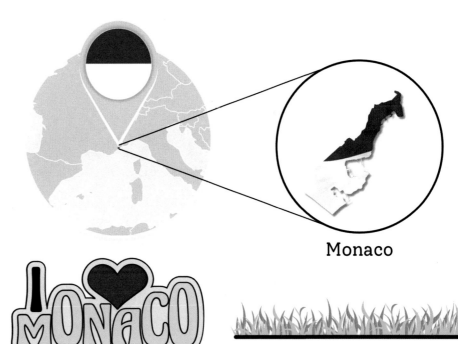

Monaco

Copyright @2023 James K. Mahi

Monaco is **the second smallest country in the world,** after Vatican City.

It is located on **the French Riviera in Western Europe.**

Which continent does Monaco belong to?
- Monaco is located in Europe.

How many countries does Monaco border?
- Monaco shares its border with only one country, and that is France.

What is the official name of Monaco?
- The official name of Monaco is the "Principality of Monaco."

What are the people of Monaco called?
- The people of Monaco are called "Monégasque" or "Monegasque."

How big is Monaco?
- Monaco covers an area of approximately 2.02 square kilometers (0.78 square miles), making it one of the smallest countries in the world.

What is the population of Monaco?
- Monaco had a population of around 36,297 people.

Is Monaco overly populated?
- Yes, Monaco is one of the most densely populated countries in the world.

What percentage of the world's land does Monaco occupy?
- Monaco occupies an extremely small percentage of the world's land, less than 0.001%.

How many time zones are there in Monaco?
- Monaco operates in the Central European Time (CET) zone, which is UTC+1, and Central European Summer Time (CEST) during daylight saving, which is UTC+2.

What is Monaco's nickname?
- Monaco is often referred to as the "Playground of the Rich."

Who ruled Monaco first?
- The Grimaldi family has ruled Monaco since the 13th century.

What is the oldest city in Monaco?

- Monaco itself is the oldest city in the principality.

Which months are the coldest in Monaco?

- The coldest months in Monaco are typically December, January, and February.

Which months are the hottest in Monaco?

- The hottest months in Monaco are usually July and August.

What was the old name of Monaco?

- The old name of Monaco was "Monoecus" in ancient times.

Why do tourists visit Monaco?

- Tourists visit Monaco for its luxurious lifestyle, casinos, Formula 1 Grand Prix, beautiful beaches, and cultural attractions.

How many visitors visit Monaco every year?

- Monaco attracts millions of visitors each year, but the exact number may vary from year to year.

Monaco is known for its luxurious lifestyle and is often associated with wealth and glamour.

Monaco has a population of around 36,297 people, making it one of the most densely populated countries in the world.

The official language of Monaco is French, but Italian and English are also widely spoken.

The country is ruled by a prince, and Prince Albert II has been the reigning monarch since 2005.

Monaco is famous for its annual Formula 1 Grand Prix, held on the streets of Monte Carlo.

The Monaco Grand Prix circuit is one of the most challenging in Formula 1 racing due to its narrow streets and sharp turns.

It is also known for its glamorous casinos, including the famous Casino de Monte-Carlo.

TAXES

Monaco is a tax haven, and many wealthy individuals and businesses choose to reside there due to its low taxes.

The Monaco has no income tax, which makes it particularly attractive to the rich and famous.

Monaco has a beautiful Mediterranean climate with mild winters and warm summers.

The Grimaldi family has ruled Monaco for over 700 years.

The Monaco is famous for its annual Red Cross Ball, which is attended by celebrities and royalty from around the world.

Monaco is home to the Oceanographic Museum, founded by Prince Albert I in 1910.

The Monaco is known for its beautiful gardens, including the Exotic Garden and the Princess Grace Rose Garden.

Monaco is a constitutional monarchy with a parliamentary system.

Monaco is not a member of the European Union but uses the euro (EUR) as its official currency.

Monaco has a high standard of living, with excellent healthcare and education systems.

The official religion of Monaco is Roman Catholicism.

The Monaco is famous for its luxury yachts, which can often be seen in the harbor.

Monaco is home to the Monte Carlo Ballet and the Monte Carlo Philharmonic Orchestra.

The Monaco Grand Prix is one of the oldest and most prestigious car races in the world, first held in 1929.

Monaco is a monarchy, but it also has a constitution that was adopted in 1962. This means that Monaco has a system of government that combines the elements of a hereditary monarchy and a representative democracy.

The national day of Monaco is celebrated on November 19th. It is the day of Saint Rainier III, who was the prince of Monaco from 1949 to 2005.

Monaco is known for its beautiful beaches, including Larvotto Beach and Monte Carlo Beach.

The Prince's Palace of Monaco is a historic landmark and the official residence of the ruling monarch.

Monaco's economy relies heavily on tourism, banking, and finance.

The Monaco has its own postage stamps, which are highly collectible.

Monaco is famous for its luxurious shopping districts, including the Golden Circle of luxury boutiques.

There are no airports in Monaco, but the nearest international airport is in Nice, France.

The Monaco is known for its annual International Circus Festival,
attracting circus performers from around the world.

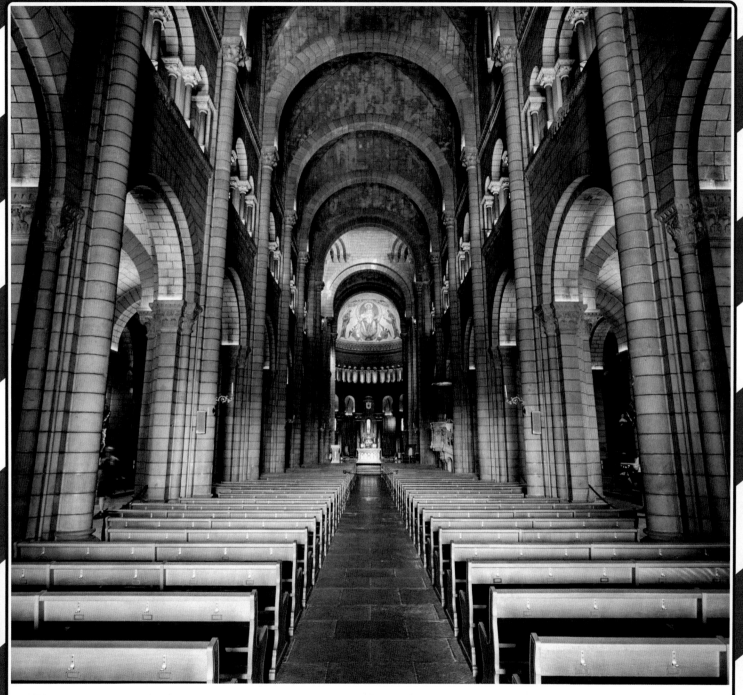

The country is home to many beautiful historic churches and cathedrals, including the Saint Nicholas Cathedral.

The Monaco is famous for its high-end restaurants, with many Michelin-starred chefs calling Monaco home.

Monaco is known for its stunning views of the Mediterranean Sea from its elevated position on the French Riviera.

Monaco's flag consists of two horizontal bands, red on top and white on the bottom.

Monaco's national anthem is called "Hymne Monégasque."

Ecole française
French school

The official language of instruction in Monaco's schools is French.

Monaco's royal family is one of the wealthiest in the world, thanks to its ownership of various businesses and properties.

Despite its small size, Monaco offers a wide range of cultural events, including art exhibitions, concerts, and festivals throughout the year.

Monaco hosts the annual Monte Carlo Rally, one of the oldest and most prestigious rallies in the world.

Monaco's national football team, AS Monaco FC, competes in France's Ligue 1.

Monaco has a strong commitment to environmental conservation and has been working to reduce its carbon footprint.

TOP 10 MONACO TRAVEL TIPS:

1. Pack Smart: Monaco is known for its fancy places, so pack some smart and stylish clothes.
2. Currency: Monaco uses the euro, so bring some euros or a credit card for shopping and dining.
3. Public Transport: Use buses or trains to get around; they're efficient and more budget-friendly than taxis.
4. Explore on Foot: Monaco is tiny, so walking is a great way to see everything up close.
5. Visit Casinos: Even if you don't gamble, visit the famous Casino de Monte-Carlo for its beautiful architecture.
6. Respect Dress Code: Some places like the casino have a dress code, so check before you go.
7. Enjoy Local Cuisine: Try Monaco's delicious seafood and French cuisine in local restaurants.
8. Safety: Monaco is very safe, but keep an eye on your belongings in crowded areas.
9. Language: French is the main language, but English is widely understood, so no worries about language barriers.
10. Plan Ahead: Monaco can be expensive, so plan your budget in advance.

PROS OF VISITING MONACO:

- **Luxury:** Experience the glamorous and luxurious lifestyle of the rich and famous.
- **Beautiful Scenery:** Enjoy stunning Mediterranean views, beautiful gardens, and charming streets.
- **Cultural Attractions:** Explore museums, historic sites, and cultural events.
- **Safety:** Monaco is one of the safest places in the world, making it ideal for travelers.
- **Delicious Food:** Savor delicious French and Mediterranean cuisine at local restaurants.

CONS OF VISITING MONACO:

- **Expensive:** Monaco is one of the priciest destinations, so be prepared for high costs.
- **Small Size:** It's a tiny country, so you can explore it quickly, and some may find it too small.
- **Crowds:** During peak tourist season, Monaco can be crowded, making it less peaceful.
- **Limited Beaches:** Monaco's beaches are small and can get crowded quickly.
- **Parking and Traffic:** Finding parking and dealing with traffic in the city can be challenging.

Made in United States
Orlando, FL
11 November 2024

53751867R00024